CLEOPATRA

— QUEEN OF EGYPT —

CLEOPATRA
QUEEN OF EGYPT

XINA M. UHL

Educational Publishing

IN ASSOCIATION WITH

EDUCATIONAL SERVICES

Published in 2018 by Britannica Educational Publishing (a trademark of Encyclopædia Britannica, Inc.) in association with The Rosen Publishing Group, Inc.
29 East 21st Street, New York, NY 10010

Distributed exclusively by Rosen Publishing.
To see additional Britannica Educational Publishing titles, go to rosenpublishing.com.

First Edition

Britannica Educational Publishing
J.E. Luebering: Executive Director, Core Editorial
Andrea R. Field: Managing Editor, Compton's by Britannica

Rosen Publishing
Heather Moore Niver: Editor
Nelson Sá: Art Director
Michael Moy: Designer
Cindy Reiman: Photography Manager
Heather Moore Niver: Photo Researcher

Library of Congress Cataloging-in-Publication Data

Names: Uhl, Xina M., author.
Title: Cleopatra : Queen of Egypt / Xina M. Uhl.
Description: First edition. | New York : Britannica Educational Publishing in association with Rosen Educational Services, 2018. | Series: Women who changed history | Includes bibliographical references and index.
Identifiers: LCCN 2016057941| ISBN 9781680486391 (library bound : alkaline paper) | ISBN 9781680486377 (paperback : alkaline paper) | ISBN 9781680486384 (6-pack : alkaline paper)
Subjects: LCSH: Cleopatra, Queen of Egypt, -30 B.C.—Juvenile literature. | Queens—Egypt—Biography—Juvenile literature. | Egypt—Kings and rulers—Biography—Juvenile literature. | Egypt—History—332-30 B.C.—Juvenile literature.
Classification: LCC DT92.7 .U33 2018 | DDC 932.021092 [B] —dc23
LC record available at https://lccn.loc.gov/2016057941

Manufactured in the United States of America

CONTENTS

INTRODUCTION

Cleopatra is one of the most famous women from ancient history, and for good reason. As the queen of Egypt, she ruled the richest nation that bordered the Mediterranean Sea. But she lost that throne at age twenty-one when she was driven into exile by her brother's supporters and forced to flee Egypt for Syria. She only regained the throne through an alliance to a powerful Roman named Julius Caesar. Once she was restored to her throne, however, the drama did not end. It continued with the murder of one and possibly two of her brothers, clever plotting by Cleopatra to increase Egypt's fortunes, and armed conflict that ended in her death.

At a time when Egypt's rulers distanced themselves from their subjects, Cleopatra did not. She was the only member of her family to learn the Egyptian language. In her portraits, she appeared wearing Egyptian dress. One of her titles was *Philopatris*, a word that means "she who loves her country." This love was returned by the Egyptian people, among whom she was greatly popular.

As a woman ruler she made full use of all her gifts as a person and a descendant of her royal family. Plutarch, a biographer from antiquity, described her as charming, irresistible, and bewitching. She was not a great beauty, he said, but her presence alone impressed everyone. When she spoke, "It was a pleasure merely to hear the sound of her voice, with which, like an instrument of many strings, she could pass from one language to another." In fact, Cleopatra spoke nine languages in all.

Though many people today remember Cleopatra for her beauty and charm, she was also a powerful ruler who did not hesitate to order the deaths of her enemies.

Cleopatra was not only smart and daring, but ruthless and murderous. Like other rulers in the ancient world, she sent countless soldiers to die in her wars. She sacrificed some of her own family to her ambitions as well.

During Cleopatra's lifetime (69–30 BCE), Egypt was more than a fabulously wealthy country. It was also the last of the nations of the Mediterranean to keep its independence from the Roman Empire. Rome, the seat of the Roman Empire, lies in the middle of the Italian peninsula. From here streamed legions of soldiers. They conquered modern-day North Africa, Greece, the Balkans, Germany, France, Spain, and Britain. One of these conquerors, Julius Caesar, would play a large part in Cleopatra's life. So would Caesar's companion, a powerful Roman general named Mark Antony. Antony became Cleopatra's husband and the father to three of her children.

She used all her power to keep Egypt free of Rome's greedy grasp. In the end, her gamble failed. When Julius Caesar was murdered, civil war broke out. Soon after, Rome declared war on Egypt. Cleopatra and Mark Antony joined their navies to fight a legendary battle. They lost. Both ended up dying by suicide.

In the years since her death, the memory of Cleopatra has lived on. She has been a subject of poems, plays, books, art, and films. However, her fascinating true story rivals the fiction.

CHAPTER ONE

DAUGHTER
OF THE NILE

Alexander der Große vor Tyros. Zeichnung von H. Vogel.

In the fourth century BCE a conqueror emerged from the rocky highlands of what is today Macedonia. Alexander the Great (b. 356 BCE–d. 323 BCE) and his army of Greeks swept through the Mediterranean world. They conquered land east across Asia Minor, the Middle East, and all the way to India. To the south, they defeated and ruled Egypt. Alexander founded cities along the way. One of those was Alexandria, on the northern coast of Egypt. It sat at the mouth of the mighty Nile River.

Alexander died in 323 BCE without leaving a successor to his empire. His four generals

Alexander the Great ordered a causeway to connect the island of Tyre with the mainland and sent his armies over it to conquer the city. The causeway remains in place today.

9

ALEXANDRIA

In 332 BCE, Alexander the Great came to Rhakotis, a small port village near the sea. He changed the town's name to Alexandria, and made plans to build a magnificent city in its place. Its location near the sea allowed it to become a center of trade for goods from Arabia and India. Papyrus, glass, metal, and textiles were produced there.

Trade brought wealth. The population grew so that it became the largest city in the Mediterranean, and Alexandria became the capital of Egypt. The arts flourished. Schools of philosophy sprang up. Scholars of all kinds gathered there, including Jewish translators, who created a Greek version of the Old Testament from the original Hebrew.

Two of Alexandria's buildings were famous. One is the great Library. It housed up to 500,000 papyrus scrolls. (Books such as we know them were a later invention.) Alexandria's lighthouse, Pharos, was one of the Seven Wonders of the Ancient World. It was said to stand about 440 feet (134 meters) tall. Sailors could see its light up to 35 miles (about 56 kilometers) out at sea.

Over time, both the lighthouse and library were destroyed. In the seventh century Muslim Arabs conquered the city. In the sixteenth

Macedonia, 336 BC
Alexander's empire at its height, 323 BC
• Cities

century epidemics of disease dwindled the population. But by the nineteenth century, Alexandria had recovered to become a major center for cotton production. The city remains to this day, and functions as a popular spot for tourists. In 2006, it had a population of more than four million.

© 2006 Encyclopædia Britannica, Inc.

Egypt was a small part of Alexander the Great's empire, which spread Greek culture from Macedonia all the way across the Indus River to the east.

divided up his empire and ruled it. Ptolemy was the name of the general who took over Egypt. He established a dynasty of the same name there. Egypt reached the height of its glory from 285 to 246 BCE. Afterward, a long age of war and fighting within the country caused it to decline.

THE PTOLEMIES

While the Ptolemies ruled Egypt for nearly three hundred years, they never really became Egyptians. Instead, they remained Greek. They did not marry outside the family. Unlike today, this was accepted practice. Brothers and sisters married. So did uncles and nieces or cousins. They did this to keep their wealth and power within the family. Family marriages took place among the gods of Egypt and Greece, too. When it came to their traditions and the language they spoke, the Ptolemies were Greek, not Egyptian. They stayed apart from their people in the city of Alexandria.

The Egyptian army during this period had few native men in it. It was filled almost entirely with Greeks or Macedonians. The same was true of important government offices.

Each of the kings were called Ptolemy, and each queen was named either Cleopatra or Berenice. Historians have assigned Roman numerals to them in order to keep track of who was who throughout the years.

THE SEVEN CLEOPATRAS

Cleopatra VII was the last in a long line of Cleopatras.

Cleopatra I Syra lived between 215 and 176 BCE. She might have been named after Alexander the Great's sister. When her husband died, she served as regent for her elder son. After her death, he took the title Philometor. It means "mother-loving."

Cleopatra II (circa 185–116 BCE) was Cleopatra I's daughter. She married two of her brothers, Ptolemy VI and Ptolemy VIII. Her husband-brother Ptolemy VIII then married her daughter, Cleopatra III (circa 160/155–101 BCE). Mother and daughter quarreled, and in 132–130 BCE Cleopatra II fled to Syria. She later went to war against her husband-brother and her daughter. The family

Though she came from a long line of Greeks, Cleopatra took care to dress in a manner that celebrated her Egyptian roots.

(continued on the next page)

(continued from the previous page)

reconciled in about 124 BCE. They ruled together until Ptolemy's death in 116 BCE. Cleopatra II died soon after.

After the death of her parents, Cleopatra III ruled with her elder son. Then, from 107 BCE on, she ruled with her younger son. She served as a priestess in the royal court. Her younger son is said to have ordered her death on October 26, 101 BCE.

Cleopatra IV (c. 140–112 BCE), daughter of Cleopatra III, followed in her mother's footsteps by marrying her brother. He divorced her and she married the king of Syria. Two years later, her sister ordered her killed.

The identities of Cleopatra V and VI are uncertain. Some sources say that Cleopatra V Selene (135–69 BCE) was another daughter of Cleopatra III. This Cleopatra married four times, once to a brother. The king of Armenia is thought to have ordered her killed in 69 BCE. Cleopatra Tryphaena is sometimes known as Cleopatra V and other times as Cleopatra VI. She lived between 95 and 55 BCE. Little else is known about her.

CLEOPATRA IS BORN

Cleopatra's full name is Cleopatra VII Thea Philopator, or "Cleopatra the Father-Loving Goddess." She was born in 70/69 BCE, the second oldest of six children. Her father

The sphinx shown here is thought to have the head of Ptolemy XII, Cleopatra's father. Sphinxes were mythical creatures with the body of a lion and a human head.

was Ptolemy XII and the identity of her mother is a mystery, though some believe that it is Cleopatra Tryphaena.

Her father tried to keep his throne and retain Egypt's independence from Rome by the use of bribes. His submission to Rome angered the people of Alexandria, who drove him out of Egypt. Cleopatra may have joined him.

In 58 BCE the Egyptians crowned Cleopatra's mother and her eldest sister, Berenice IV, rulers. Cleopatra's mother soon died, and some believe that Berenice poisoned her. Berenice became sole ruler. She did not keep her position long. By 55 BCE, Ptolemy returned to Egypt with a Roman army and regained his throne. He executed Berenice. Ptolemy died in 51. Just before this, he made Cleopatra and her brother Ptolemy XIII co-rulers.

It is clear that as Cleopatra grew to adulthood, she faced family strife. But a series of problems also plagued Egypt itself. Rome pressured it from the outside, much of the land it had previously owned had been lost, and a famine caused misery and death.

Cleopatra's upbringing must have been challenging. However, it also prepared her for the chaos she would soon face.

CHAPTER TWO

A YOUNG QUEEN

At about eighteen years of age, Cleopatra became queen of Egypt. Before this, she may have briefly acted as her father's co-ruler. Her father died in February or March 51 BCE. Shortly before then, he appointed Cleopatra and her ten-year-old brother Ptolemy XIII Egypt's next rulers. She and her brother may have married after this. They probably had little love for one another, though.

CLEOPATRA TAKES POWER

Cleopatra acted quickly to assert her power. On

Eliz. Cheron I.H. delin.   *J. de la Croix sculp.*

Portrait du Jeune Ptolomée dernier Roi d'Egypte tiré d'un Médaillon Antique d'argent

Avec Privil. du Roi

The antique silver medallion shown here represents Ptolemy XIII, the short-lived brother of Cleopatra.

March 22, 51 BCE, she sailed up the Nile river to the city of Hermonthis. There, she installed a new sacred bull. Egyptians worshiped many animals as part of the practice of various animal cults that existed at the time. The bull cult was one of these. Cleopatra may have been the first of the Ptolemaic rulers to attend this ceremony in person.

In fact, she performed many firsts as a ruler. She was the first to learn the Egyptian language. Her official portraits show her wearing Egyptian dress. She took this journey to Hermonthis with at least two purposes in mind. One, she wanted to show the Egyptian people that she was their new queen. Second, she wanted to gather power for herself. Her plans worked. Soon,

By leaving her brother and co-ruler's name off her decrees Cleopatra let her ambition to rule alone show itself.

WOMEN IN EGYPT

Women who lived in the world of ancient Mesopotamia often had little power of their own. That was not the case in Egypt, though. Women in Egypt could decide whom they wanted to marry. They could own their own property, and inherit amounts equal to men. A married woman did not have to live under the control of her husband. She could even divorce him if she so chose. Women could own businesses and serve as priestesses in temples. In fact, up to one third of the land during Cleopatra's time may have been held by women. Foreigners who visited Egypt were shocked by the rights that the women there enjoyed.

she signed decrees in her own name, leaving off her brother's name entirely.

Ptolemy XIII and his supporters objected to her power grab. They forced Cleopatra into exile in 48 BCE. She fled to Syria, where she raised an army. The forces of Ptolemy XIII and Cleopatra fought at the city of Pelusium in eastern Egypt.

Meanwhile, a power struggle was also playing out in Rome. Former allies General Pompey and Julius Caesar became rivals. Pompey fled Rome and arrived in Pelusium. There, he sought protection from Ptolemy XIII. Pompey had no more arrived on the shore of Ptolemy's camp than he was murdered.

Ptolemy XIII thought that by murdering Pompey he would gain favor with Julius Caesar. When presented with Pompey's head, Caesar burst into tears.

Three days later, Julius Caesar arrived in Alexandria. Riots in the streets greeted him. The Egyptian fleet in the harbor trapped him and his four thousand troops. To break open this blockade, he ordered his men to set fire to the Egyptian ships. The fire got out of control, though, and destroyed warehouses, depots, and other buildings. One of those is believed to have been the great Library of Alexandria.

As the leader of Rome, Caesar wanted the fighting between Cleopatra and her brother to cease. He called them both to come to him.

Julius Caesar had an eventful life as a Roman soldier and statesman. Before he was dictator, he was once held captive by pirates and he also served briefly as the governor of a province of Spain.

Cleopatra, eager to regain the throne, decided to make Caesar her ally. To do that, she had to enact a daring plan.

THE WOMAN HERSELF

The ancient sources that talk about Cleopatra tell us the things that she did. But they say little about who she was as a person. Still, we can surmise some things about her.

As a royal daughter, Cleopatra had a good education, unlike many of the common people. A man named Philostratos taught her philosophy, rhetoric, and oratory. Like many educated people of the day, she became a writer. Her skill with languages made her special—she is said to have spoken nine of them. The poems, stories, and films written about her after her death speak about her great beauty. The truth is that her looks were not as impressive as her charisma.

Actress Evelyn Brent portrays Cleopatra in this photo, showing how 1920s Hollywood conceived of her.

CLEOPATRA THE WRITER

During ancient times, members of the ruling classes often composed their own writings. Ptolemy I, Cleopatra's ancestor, published a history of Alexander the Great. Ptolemy VIII wrote a memoir twenty-four books long. Due to her education and family history, Cleopatra would have been expected to create scholarly works.

Several fragments of her writings have survived to the present day. They all seem to come from a work called *The Cosmetics*. The medical subjects it covered include remedies for baldness and dandruff. It also provided eight treatments for a disease called "fox-mange" that causes the hair to fall out. Other fragments reveal a recipe for perfumed soap and a guide on how to curl and dye the hair. Recipes and medical treatments would have required accurate amounts of ingredients. Because of this, *The Cosmetics* also had a long section on weights and measures.

Like other Egyptian rulers, she believed that she was divine. She identified with the goddesses Isis and Aphrodite. The moon represented Isis. In Egyptian belief, Isis was the wife of the god of the sun, Osiris. She was associated with medicine and farming. Aphrodite was a Greek goddess of love, beauty, and fertility. The Romans called this goddess Venus.

Cleopatra used disguises, costumes, and shows of splendor to accomplish her aims. Her later deeds display her

This relief shows Cleopatra as the goddess Isis. Isis was believed to be a healer, mother, and wife and was a role model for Egyptian women.

strength, intelligence, and ambition. But she could also be ruthless and murderous. These qualities combined with her love for Egypt. They drove her to ally herself with powerful Roman men like Julius Caesar to keep Egypt safe and to make it prosper.

CHAPTER THREE

DANGER AND DESIRE

Caesar had set up his residence in the royal palace at Alexandria. From there, he called for Cleopatra and her co-ruling brother to come to him. He wanted for them to settle their dispute. One reason for this is that Rome depended on Egypt for its supply of grain for bread.

Cleopatra knew that she would have a better chance of Rome siding with her if she managed to plead her case with Caesar before her brother could. But there was a problem. His army kept her out of Egypt entirely. So she came up with a plan. Secretly, she and her loyal friends sailed a little boat down the Nile River. The trip took eight days. When they got to Alexandria, night had fallen. Her servant Apollodorus docked the boat. Cleopatra either climbed into a large sack or rolled herself up in a carpet. Apollodorus then carried her over his shoulder and into the palace. He told Caesar that he was bringing a gift, so he took the carpet right into Caesar's room.

Then, Cleopatra rolled out of the carpet, surprising Caesar. Her ruse worked. Caesar was charmed and sided with Cleopatra over her brother. She was now home from exile

Cleopatra emerging from a carpet in front of Julius Caesar is a favorite subject of artists and playwrights alike.

JULIUS CAESAR

One of the most famous men in world history, Julius Caesar was born around 100 BCE. He held a number of offices in Rome's government, including military ones. Caesar and his army conquered much of central Europe (called Gaul at the time) for Rome. He also attacked Britain. In 51 BCE he published *The Gallic Wars*, his history of his military triumphs in Gaul, Germany, and Britain.

In 49 BCE he led his armies across the Rubicon River toward Rome. By crossing the Rubicon with an army he was declaring civil war. His forces won the war and he became dictator of Rome in 46 BCE. This position allowed him to rule alone.

When he met Cleopatra, he was fifty-two years old. She was around twenty-one. Despite their age difference, he found her captivating. This was due, in part, to her intelligence and education.

The historian Suetonius provides a look at Caesar. "He was tall, of a fair complexion, round limbed, rather full faced, with eyes black and piercing; he enjoyed excellent health except toward the close of his life when he was subject to sudden fainting fits and disturbances in his sleep."

Caesar was known as a ladies' man. He cared about his looks. He even went so far as to wear a laurel wreath on his head to cover his bald spot.

and back on the throne. Another younger brother, Ptolemy XIV, became both her co-ruler and her new husband.

Despite the fact that Julius Caesar and Cleopatra were both married to other people, they became a couple. They

This relief on the Temple of Hathor in Dendera, Egypt, shows
Cleopatra and her son Caesarion presenting offerings to the gods.

spent the winter together in Alexandria. The next spring, Roman troops arrived to assist Caesar in the fight against Ptolemy XIII. In the course of fleeing this army, Ptolemy XIII drowned in the Nile River. He was only about fifteen years old at the time of his death in 47 BCE.

In June 47 BCE Cleopatra gave birth to Ptolemy Caesar. To the people of Alexandria he was known as Caesarion, or "little Caesar." Cleopatra claimed that Julius Caesar was his father, but no one knows for certain if this is true.

THE VISIT TO ROME

After eighteen months spent in Egypt, Julius Caesar returned home to Rome. There, he discovered that his rivals had gone to Africa to raise an army against him. He traveled to Africa in 46 BCE and defeated them. Next, he went to Spain where he defeated other rivals.

In the meantime, Cleopatra and Caesarion went to Rome, where they stayed at Caesar's villa. He

Julius Caesar was assassinated on March 15, 44 BCE. The fifteenth of March was known as the Ides of March, a day of Roman religious festivities.

visited them frequently. In February 44 BCE, Caesar named himself dictator for life. One month later, a group of Roman senators assassinated him. Cleopatra returned to Egypt. Soon after, Ptolemy XIV died, most likely poisoned by Cleopatra.

ANOTHER ROMAN MAN

Cleopatra's dealings with Rome were not through. After Caesar's death, Rome broke into civil war. The Roman Empire was split into east and west. The ruler of the east was Mark Antony, a former ally of Caesar's. His armies had chased down Caesar's assassins. However, he had heard reports that Cleopatra had aided his enemies. In 41 BCE he ordered her to appear before him at Tarsus in Asia Minor.

Their meeting is one of the most famous in history.

Cleopatra floated down the Cydnus River on a luxurious barge. The barge sported purple sails, a gilded stern, and silver oars. On the deck, musicians played flutes, pipes, and lyres. She reclined under a golden canopy, dressed as Venus, the Roman goddess of love. Young boys painted like Cupid fanned her. And her maids dressed like sea nymphs. Incense hung in sweet-smelling clouds.

The display dazzled Mark Antony. On shore, Cleopatra prepared a number of banquets. She and Antony dined on tables with gold plates. She likely wore pearls and precious

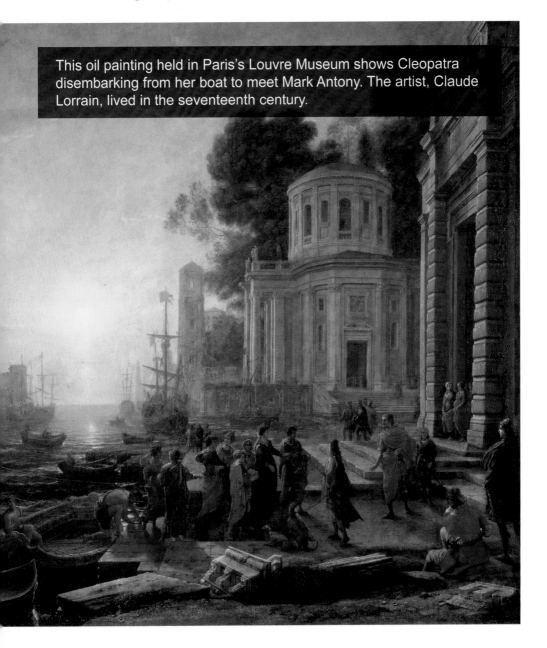

This oil painting held in Paris's Louvre Museum shows Cleopatra disembarking from her boat to meet Mark Antony. The artist, Claude Lorrain, lived in the seventeenth century.

gems. Lights hung in the tree branches nearby. Perfume scented the air and at one point, rose petals covered the floor knee-deep.

Like she had done with Caesar before him, Cleopatra cast her spell on Antony. At first, at least, she did so to keep her beloved Egypt safe. She must have fallen for Antony as well, though. He soon followed her back to Alexandria. The two spent a winter together.

CHAPTER FOUR

ROME TRIUMPHS

The struggles of Rome were not far away from Antony and Cleopatra, even when they lived in Egypt. Julius Caesar did not have any children to hand over his throne to. He solved that problem by adopting a young man named Octavian as his heir. Octavian was nineteen years old when Caesar was killed. Mark Antony competed with Octavian for power until they came up with a compromise. Octavian ruled the western Roman empire while Antony ruled the east.

Though Antony loved Cleopatra, he had duties back in Rome. He returned there and married Octavia, Octavian's sister. Cleopatra remained in Alexandria, pregnant with Antony's children. In 40 BCE she gave birth to twins named Alexander Helios and Cleopatra Selene.

For three years, Antony tried to come to terms with Octavian. In 37 BCE he decided that they could never agree, and he returned to Cleopatra. The two married. This marriage angered Octavian, who saw it as a betrayal of his sister and Antony's legal wife, Octavia.

Antony wanted Cleopatra's help to send his armies to Parthia. She agreed, but in exchange asked for the return of

This painting from the seventeenth or early eighteenth century shows a very different version of Cleopatra than the Egyptian sculpture produced while she was alive.

Egypt's former lands in Syria, Lebanon, and Jericho. In 36 BCE, Cleopatra gave birth to another of Antony's sons, Ptolemy Philadelphus.

A FAMILY OF GODS

Mark Antony's campaign in Parthia failed, though he did manage to conquer Armenia for a short time. Despite this, he and Cleopatra put together a grand celebration when he returned to Alexandria in 34 BCE. In the gymnasium, two golden thrones sat on a silver platform. Cleopatra and Antony occupied these. They portrayed themselves as divine beings. Cleopatra was the new Isis, and Antony the new Dionysos. Below them sat four thrones for their children. At the ceremony that followed, Antony awarded areas in Armenia and Cyprus to the children. He also declared that Caesarion was the son of Julius Caesar. This would make him the true heir, not Octavian.

Tensions between Egypt and Rome grew stronger. Antony and Cleopatra traveled to Greece to spend the winter of 32–31 BCE. The Roman Senate stripped Antony of his authority because they believed he had surrendered to Cleopatra. Next, they declared war on Cleopatra.

THE BATTLE OF ACTIUM

On September 2, 31 BCE, two navies met off the western coast of Greece. One belonged to Antony and Cleopatra.

They camped at Actium, where they gathered five hundred ships and seventy thousand soldiers. The other navy belonged to Octavian. He approached from the north with

Marc Antony was one of Rome's best generals. But his military skill did not save him when he and Cleopatra combined forces during the Battle of Actium.

four hundred ships and eighty thousand soldiers. The two sides met in a great naval battle. In the midst of the fighting, Cleopatra fled with her Egyptian galleys. She had

been worried about being captured. Without her, Antony's forces were not strong enough to win. Antony left the fight and followed her. The rest of his fleet, confused without a leader, surrendered to Octavian.

Cleopatra and Antony retreated to Egypt. Both she and Antony knew that Octavian would probably track them down soon, and neither one of them wanted to become a prisoner. Cleopatra collected deadly poisons, and tested them on condemned prisoners. She wanted to see which poisons caused death quickly and with little pain. The writer Plutarch claims that she settled on the bite of an asp as the perfect method of suicide.

A year after their defeat at Actium, Octavian arrived in Egypt. Alexandria fell before him. Cleopatra walled herself up in her mausoleum. There, she had collected her royal treasure of gold, silver, emeralds, pearls, ebony, ivory, and spices.

Octavian sent her a message telling her that if she killed Antony he would protect her and her family. She came up with a terrible plan to cause Antony's death. She had a message sent to Antony telling him that she had committed suicide. In grief, he fell upon his sword, but did not die right

Surrounded by the treasures in her mausoleum, Cleopatra meets with Octavian after her defeat in the Battle of Actium.

away. Instead he told his servants to take him to where Cleopatra's body lay. Instead, he found her alive. Upon seeing him, grief overtook her. He urged her to make peace with Octavian before he died.

Soon after, Octavian seized Cleopatra's mausoleum for fear that she would set it on fire. For nine days he kept her prisoner there. Octavian and Cleopatra passed messages back and forth. She hoped to find safety for herself and her children. At last, she realized that Octavian only wanted to take her and her children to Rome so they could appear in his victory parade.

This image of Cleopatra appears on a mummy's coffin from Thebes, Egypt. It dates from the second century AD, too late to be Cleopatra's actual coffin.

She allegedly had an asp brought to her hidden in a basket of figs. She made sure that the asp bit her in the chest, and she died. Other accounts say that she took poison along with her two women servants. Whatever happened, she died at thirty-nine years of age. With her died

ELIZABETH TAYLOR AS CLEOPATRA

In 1963, the four-hour-long movie *Cleopatra* was released. It starred Elizabeth Taylor as Cleopatra and Richard Burton as Mark Antony. The film cost $31 million dollars, more than any other film until that time. The high cost nearly sent its studio, 20th Century Fox, out of business. Initial reviews of the film had little good to say about it. Still, the spectacle of gold costumes, jeweled headdresses, large statues, and hundreds of extras excited viewers. So did the tale of the real-life romance between Taylor and Burton, who later married. In the end, the film won four Academy Awards, and a place in movie history.

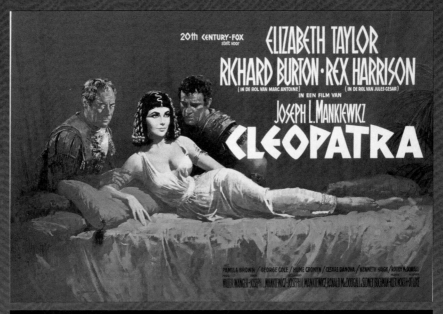

Glamorous actress Elizabeth Taylor is still remembered for her role as Cleopatra in the lavish production released in 1963.

the Ptolemaic dynasty and Egypt's independence.

AFTERWARD

Octavian sent assassins to find Caesarion, who Cleopatra had sent east. They killed him. His death, and the death of Mark Antony, removed Octavian's last obstacles to power. He became the first Roman emperor. In 27 BCE the Roman Senate gave him the title Augustus.

Egypt had now become a province of Rome. Octavia raised Mark Antony and Cleopatra's three children to adulthood.

Augustus made sure that Roman historians and poets spoke ill of Cleopatra. They wrote that she was a wicked woman who used her beauty and charm to corrupt Roman men. As the years passed, this view of her persisted, as did her fame. She

This photo is from a 1950s production of Shakespeare's play *Antony and Cleopatra*. Cleopatra remains a popular character in plays, dramas, and literature even today.

took center stage in William Shakespeare's play *Antony and Cleopatra*. Following this, she was the subject of many plays, poetry, works of art, and operas. In the twentieth century several films were made about her.

The memory of her glamour and charm remains today. The appeal of her romances with Julius Caesar and Mark Antony cannot be denied. Yet romance is only part of the story of this powerful woman leader. The memory of her strength and daring continue on despite the fact that she lived and died more than two thousand years ago.

GLOSSARY

ally One who is associated with another as a helper and shares a common purpose.

blockade The use of troops or warships to stop people or supplies from coming and going.

campaign A series of military operations in a certain area.

charisma Special charm.

compromise To settle a dispute by giving up some demands.

cult A system of religious worship.

Cupid The Roman god of love, often portrayed as a winged naked child with a bow and arrow.

depot A place to keep goods or military supplies.

dictator A person who rules with total authority.

divine Of, relating to, or proceeding directly from God or a god.

exile To force someone to leave their country.

famine A great shortage of food.

galley A type of ship moved by oars.

gymnasium An exercise ground or school.

legion A group of soldiers.

mausoleum A large tomb.

oratory The art of speaking.

papyrus Parts of a plant that are mashed, made into strips, and pressed into a writing material.

philosophy Basic ideas about truth, right and wrong, and the meaning of life.

rhetoric The art of speaking or writing effectively.

ruse A trick.

successor A person that follows another one to a throne.

villa A large expensive house in the country.

FOR FURTHER READING

Art, Suzanne Strauss. *Early Times: The Story of Ancient Rome.* Freeport, ME: Wayside Publishing, 2012.

Boyer, Crispin. *Everything Ancient Egypt.* Des Moines, IA: National Geographic Children's Books, 2012.

eKids. *A Kid's Guide to Cleopatra: A Book Just for Kids.* CreateSpace Independent Publishing Platform, 2014.

Medina, Nico. *Who Was Julius Caesar?* New York, NY: Grosset & Dunlap, 2014.

Norwich, Grace. *I Am Cleopatra.* New York, NY: Scholastic Paperbacks, 2014.

Pack, Mary Fisk. *Cleopatra: "Serpent of the Nile."* Foster City, CA: Goosebottom Books, 2011.

Pocket Genius: Ancient Egypt. New York, NY: DK Children, 2016.

Shecter, Vicky Alvear. *Cleopatra Rules!: The Amazing Life of the Original Teen Queen.* Honesdale, PA: Boyds Mills Press, 2013.

WEBSITES

Because of the changing nature of internet links, Rosen Publishing has developed an online list of websites related to the subject of this book. This site is updated regularly. Please use this link to access this list:

http://www.rosenlinks.com/WWCH/cleopatra

INDEX